# Advanced Social Jujitsu

By James Nugent

## Introduction

This book can stand alone but if you plan on being a completely effective Social Jujitsu practitioner you will need to add the tools demonstrated in the first book. The Book is called "Social Jujitsu and Powerful Principles for Managing Social Conflict" by James Nugent. It teaches the three key strategies of: evading, deflecting, and redirecting social aggressors. This book moves on to teach about drawing the aggressor in getting them to react to you, putting the aggressor in a double bind, and helping them self-destruct.

## Warning

These techniques are not to be used casually. They can occasionally escalate a situation and if you don't know other social jujitsu strategies, it can get out of your control. If at any time you feel in danger in a social conflict immediately leave and or call the police. No system of self-defense can guarantee your wellbeing.

## Disclaimer

You are the only one who is responsible for your choices in relationship and life. This book is not in any way a substitute for competent mental health consultation or therapy. If you need help in dealing your relationships get help from a professional. This booklet is just for discussion purposes only.

## Part One

-Action is stronger than reaction.

I will use examples from real combat as illustrations/analogies for the following basic concept in social jujitsu.

It is more efficient and often more effective to have a social aggressor reacting to you instead of you reacting to him/her. Just like in a fist fight. If you can take a shot at a pressure point before they land a punch, you have the advantage. You can break away or finish the fight.

Example

A street fighter moves in with his fist drawn back ready to strike at your face. Holding your ground, you place your hands half way to the targets with arms half-cocked and palms facing the attacker. Your primary weapons are now 12" from his face. If he even flinches and starts to take the punch at you; you may strike at his throat before he can land the punch which must travel at least 2' to its target.

Example from Real Life

In real life, in a bathroom a drunk had me confused with someone else. As he moved in and began a wild round house punch to my face; I raise my hands to the defensive position with both palms facing him. Then I hit him with: a spear hand to the throat, a cupped hand slap to his ear drum, and a palm strike to the tip of his chin.

I don't know which strike knocked him out, but he fell gently into my arms and I sat him against the wall.  I avoided the blood coming out of his ear. I called an ambulance for him and he never remembered what happened.

It was much safer for both of us if he never landed the first punch.

In social jujitsu we don't draw blood.

Example for Social Jujitsu

You are at a family event when the notorious family gossip and liar sits next to you. She moves in with, "Did you hear about Anne calling the police on her husban...." At the point you take the initiative and strike. You say, "You know if you weren't such a liar I would let you finish your sentence." You strike again and again saying, "I don't want to hear any gossip from you. Go away."

Sandy will be stunned and embarrassed. If she doesn't go away, you can sit somewhere else. Obviously you must think of and practice your lines before the aggressor engages with you.

Example from Social Jujitsu

A notorious gossip sits down at the lunch table at work. She moves in with a question about your personal life. Before she finished her sentence you strike. You say, "I am offended by your question. This is not the place to discuss this." Then smile and change the subject.

Part of the effectiveness in this technique is the interrupting her.

Once I was verbally attacked at work by a woman whom I interrupted in her initial tirade. She fought back and said, "I am speaking." I instinctively countered with, "You may not speak to me that way, get out my office."

She was caught off guard. Nobody had ever stopped her from her abusive behavior. I documented the encounter and sent a copy to my boss. End of problem for me. She (the boss) had endless loud meetings with her.

## Example from Social Jujitsu

Somebody I was supervising felt that she was much more competent than everybody else. She verbally exploded in my face. I let her yammer on for 2 minutes and then interrupted her and said, "Is this your way of telling me you will be working somewhere else? I accept your resignation. Please give us two weeks to notice in writing and we will give you two weeks complimentary severance pay. Goodbye." I then left my office. She never returned to work. I never knew where I was going to get the complimentary severance pay!

Never go on the offense like this unless you are severing the relationship. Interrupting is quite rude.

The technique is dependent on your ability to stay very calm and strike before they can land their attack.

Basic Principles in Social Jujitsu

You are free to say virtually anything to anyone at any time.

A social aggressor takes advantage of social conventions, and the natural tendency of people to avoid conflict.

You may be rude but never abusive. For example don't name call.

Don't ever swear. This can be used against you later.

Don't get loud unless you are seeking support from a support crowd. Be careful, this may backfire.

Things to Remember in Social Jujitsu

-Remember you are in control.

-It is almost sad how much pain the social aggressor may suffer.

-Temper your behavior with mercy.

-Show no malice.

Absolutely hold no grudge. Why win the fight but lose your soul?

Once you have mastered Social Jujitsu is becomes almost fun.

## Part 2 – The Double Bind

## A Real Life Example of the Double Bind

When I was a teenager I worked at night at a grocery store. This is where I learned about the double bind. I depended on this principle for my safety for two years.

It is more difficult for a social aggressor to be hostile to someone who is kind and or compliant. The most difficult time of night was when we were closing the coolers for the night. Drunks would come in and dash to the locked coolers and yell because they were locked. Angry and drunk is a bad combination.

 I would lie to them that the manager was gone and took the key with him. Then I would lie, and say the cops had been busting drivers all night and they have been in here and across the street. Did he have anyone to call so he doesn't get busted too?

Offering the drunk the use of the phone they would immediately look out the door and say thank you. More than twice, I got there license plate number and reported them to the police.

It's hard to be mean to someone who is looking out for you! Once when I missed my shift an employee was hospitalized over an argument with a drunk over the closed and locked coolers.

I was so universally nice that when I walked out the backdoor and startled a drug dealer doing business; he grabbed me and then laugh and let me go. I apologized so profusely that he said he would always look out for me.

He said he owed me a favor just for the laughter.

Two weeks later I was putting boxes in the dumpster at night when I got jumped by three guys. My new friend beat them with a stick and made them apologize to me right there in the dimly lit parking lot.

Example from Social Jujitsu

I have many jobs that required me to be the first contact for complaints.

I always answer the phone with a cheery, "James here, how may I help you?" This stops 99% of the of the social aggressors right in their tracks. If they are one of the rare abusers who try to vent their vileness after this positive and kind greeting; I repeat my line again after a minute.

If they will not stop the aggression, I hang up. If they threatened to blow up the office or hurt people I report it to the police.

I have found that if I let people vent for even a minute they will actually become chummy and relaxed. It is a small price to pay for good will and peace.

I was once on the first day on a new job and a mom and child arrived for services. She started screaming and swearing because I had made a referral to Children's Protective Services the year previously. She was court ordered to get counseling services and had not complied. She was just days away from losing custody of her child.

She was hysterical. I stood up and said I will leave and you will never see me again, but right now what can I do to help you. She angrily told me her story. She bitterly said all her problems started when she beat her child, giving him brain damage and I reported the incident.

I referred her to a low income therapist right across the street. I listened kindly to her. Twenty minutes later she hit me on the arm, smiled and left. She got the help she needed. My supervisor gave me a raise and put me in charge of training staff in crisis intervention.

Example of Social Jujitsu

So whenever anybody has a complaint which they launch at me and I want to listen; I ask, "How so." Being defensive will not help the situation.

Once, a boss was really frustrated with my performance. I was dismayed to find out that he had given me the wrong list of responsibilities. Instead of blaming him, I let him off the hook even though I was fuming mad at because of my wasted time.

The conversation got quite collegial and I negotiated keeping all my present responsibilities and delegated all the other responsibilities to other people. It is good to be nice to the obnoxious.

Example from Social Jujitsu

The more angry the aggressor, the more kind and thoughtful I get. This has to be sincere because the aggressor will just get more enraged if they sense sarcasm.

Once I had a meeting with three peers. They were from the same department and had obviously met before the meeting to agree upon their complaints. Caught off guard and absolutely speechless to defend my actions; I dropped back to complimenting them on their perceptiveness. I thanked them and told them serious changes would happen within a week. The double bind was that I told them they were right!

In this case they were partially right but woefully wrong in so many ways. I set a time for them next meeting.

Within five days the boss decided to terminate their employments. They were not available for the next meeting. I too was disciplined. There was one valid complaint. I immediately made the correction and it was dually noted that I made the correction. Sometimes you have to just take a hit from hateful people but it can make you stronger and happier in the long run. :>

More importantly, always remember that as long as you live, the conflict is not over. Sometimes it angers your ego to hold your tongue but the wheels of justice can sometimes turn slowly. Generally you do not need to win every confrontation or conflict.

Part 3 – Self Destruction of Social Aggressors

The goal of Social Jujitsu is that you and the aggressor will become better people. However sometimes this is not a possibility within the foreseeable future.

So, we must take steps to help the aggressor destroy themselves. This is serious business and all other techniques should be use before contemplating this method.

A Note on Ethics

Make the penalty for bad behavior equal to the offense. If given superior tools do you have the right to inflict excessive punishment? NO. NO. NO.

You only have the right to stop the assault. That's it. The law in many places says the same thing.

Example from Real Life

I have a 95lb woman friend. She was once sexually assaulted by a 300lb man. She found that she could not stop the sexual assault but she decided right there and then to make sure that he could never do it again. She reached down as he was trying to rape her and pulled hard on his testicles. She removed them, and while he was bleeding, she stuck her fingers in his eyes.

She blinded him one eye and partially in the other. He was the one who pulled down his pants and he was the one who was forcing himself upon her and he was the one who paid the price. He did 5 years in prison

The point is that she didn't attack offending organ; she attacked the supporting organs that enabled him to try to rape her. His eyes and balls were fair game.

Example from Social Jujitsu

Her name was Tam. She was my boss. She wanted her nephew in my position. I needed to find a way to indirectly destroy her life. I knew that her husband was a wanted felon in another state. I talked with a friend in law enforcement and her husband was arrested and she was devastated. Not only did she lose her husband (for 18 years of prison), but she lost half her income. Soon she would lose her mortgage.

I friend who was a tank commander in the US Army taught me that in battle that the enemy cannot hit what they cannot see. There was no way that Tam could know who tattled on her husband.

Three weeks later she was back at me again. I asked her while rerecording a tape for another project, "Why she was doing this to me." She said something about how I would be happier as a store clerk. I did not know I had the recording until weeks later.

She began to micro manage me and I got help from the union. Meetings became extremely difficult for her and I called them off sometimes just to antagonize her.

Then one day I called a meeting alone. I just said that this would be the last meeting we had before we were in court. I played the accidental recording. I told her that none of this had to come to daylight as long as she agreed to not harass me. She agreed. However she still was an annoyance.

It turns out that losing a spouse (to death, divorce or other means) gives you a 300% increase in the chance of having a catastrophic medical crisis within a year. Losing the house was another stress. The crisis at work was the final straw.

She became chronically ill with a variety of stress related medical problems and went out on medical leave eight weeks later.

Note

All identifying details in this true story have been changed to protect me.

Example of Social Jujitsu

A man got in the elevator. He knew my name and what he said really upset me. He told me, he was the head of my department and he would never let me graduate from his department. He had a problem with me having multiple majors.

I told him that I would complete all the requirements and he would sign off. I was very worried. I avoided him until my graduation year. Still he harassed me in small ways.

I started a rumor in the department by telling three people that I didn't have to worry about Dr.____ because I was about to sue him and never have to work. I also sent him a letter (faked) from my deceased father demanding that this situation be remedied in a gentlemanly manner before things got litigious.

I was forced to take a seminar with him. At one time he called an emergency meeting of about 20 people, and he claimed that someone had embarrassed the department, the school and themselves. I was so very tempted to admit I was the culprit but I could not think of anything I had done. So, I did not move. After 15 seconds of silent pause two women broke-down and cried. The rest of us ran from the room. Dr. _____ had his way with two probably innocent students. They quit. I completed the program and he signed off.


Two years after I graduated I was sitting in church and I turned around and raised my hand to greet a woman I barely recognized. She was the wife of Dr.\_\_\_\_\_. She scowled at me and refused to shake my hand. Later I found out that Dr.\_\_\_\_ had had a nervous breakdown and it seemed to be centered on me. At least he mentioned my name on at least two occasions.


When a social aggressor tries to hurt you, they may be legally or psychologically vulnerable. The trick is to do your research. With the modern internet it is easy to check out an opponent but you can bluff as I did 3 decades ago, with the evil Dr._____. You can never know what is eating at them!

## Summary

These are three advance techniques at this time in Advanced Social Jujitsu. These strategies are: take action fast to get them to react to you, the double bind, and self-destruction of the aggressor. These three techniques plus the original methods of: evade, deflect and redirect; will make you a "Black Belt" in Social Jujitsu. Although Social Jujitsu will continue to evolve; these are the core concepts. Any future books will be only be variations on these founding principles.

Books by James Nugent

I Built a Raft

Advanced Social Jujitsu

Deep Catholic Morality

Paddles and Water

The Power of Habits

The Beginning School Counselor

Learning My Limits in Small Craft Boating

Eight Things You Need to Survive

Writing My First Books

How I Sailed From Olympia to the San Juan Islands, and Returned Safely

An Alternative Boating Guide to Southern Puget Sound

How and Why I lived Aboard

Kayaking Budd Inlet in South Puget Sound

Night Kayaking

Writing E-books and Making the Perfect Book

I Speak Esperanto

The Rainbow Road and Other Signs of God's Love

Living an Abundant Life, Within Your Means

Social Jujitsu and Powerful Principles for Managing Social Conflict

Blackjack on My Small Budget

A Little Benedictine Oblate Manuel

Without Speech

All things work

Loving Time with Your Creator

Personal Adventures in a Life of Learning

The Good News about Being Catholic

E-book Writing and Overcoming Barriers to Creativity

E-book Writing and Organizing Your Ideas

My Forty Days for Life 2013

Lifestyle Reality Observing

How to Sail in the Winter

How to Get Your Kid to Move Out

How to Get What Want

Sex, Abstinence, and Happiness

Cynthia Says Radio Show – Anger is a choice

More Good News about Being Catholic

The Solo Kayak

A Beach Naturalist on Southern Puget Sound

Clean House Clean Life

The Total Catholic Christian

Happiness is a Choice

Solo Kayak II

The Extraordinary Eucharistic Visitor

The Catholic Way of Dying

*Available at Amazon.com in Kindle E-Book and or Audible Book or Paperback*

www.ingramcontent.com/pod-product-compliance
Lightning Source LLC
Chambersburg PA
CBHW061948280526
45787CB00004B/1774